"Plant Bird"   Proof   Oeshach '69

Shifting Tenses for a Friend

(for Nelson Oestreich)

I am preparing a manuscript
to interest a publisher
in our book
Bird by Bird Watching,
Nelson's woodblock prints
and my poems
with an introduction
by Kerri and Adam Duerr
two young ornithologists
who know something
about birds.

  When Nelson died
I had to change the verbs
in "About the Artist"
from the past progressive
to the simple past.
It wasn't simple
and it made my loss
as real as the boots
Nelson's son Eric nailed
to a tree in the woods
because Nelson
didn't need them
anymore.

James A. Perkins
July 1, 2015

Bird by Bird Watching

'Men work together,' I told him from the heart,
'Whether they work together or apart.'

Robert Frost "The Tuft of Flowers"

Bird by Bird Watching

Woodblock Prints
by
Nelson E. Oestreich

Poems
by
James A. Perkins

with an introduction
by
Kerri and Adam Duerr

First Printing, 2016

Dawn Valley Press
P.O. Box 112
Beaver, PA 15009
DawnValleyPress.com

ISBN: 978-0-936014-05-0
ebook ISBN: 978-0-936014-08-1

Cover design and layout: Anna Buzzelli (buzzellidesign.com)

Acknowledgments

The following poems have appeared, sometimes in a slightly different form, in the magazines listed below. I am grateful to these journals for their support of poetry in general and of my work in particular.

"Bird Dog," *The Black Fly Review* 6 1985: 20.

"Dalliance," *The Cape Rock* 22.1 Spring, 1987: 7.

"Dressing the Bride of Spring," *Zuzu's Petals Quarterly* 2.1 Winter/Spring, 1993: 29.

"Except for the Gull," *The Princeton Packet* "Time Off" 8 April 1987: 32.

"Hawks Drop Restless onto Air," *The Southern Review* 92.1 Winter, 1996: 49.

"Invisible Deaths," *Colorado Review*, New Series 13.1 Fall 1985: 72.

"A Poem about a Goose," *Patterson Literary Review* Patterson, NJ: Passaic County Community College, 1993: 38.

"Remembering the Field of Blackbirds," *The Southern Review* 92.1 Winter, 1996: 47-48.

"Remembering Through The Blood," Footwork: *The Patterson Literary Review* '88: 38.

"Searching for Blue," *U.S. 1 Worksheets* 40/41 1999: 20.

"The Possibility of the Lesser Blue Heron," *The Black Fly Review* 14 1993: 37.

"The Sound of My Brush," *U.S. 1 Worksheets* 24/25 Spring, 1991: 20.

"Who We Are," *The Black Fly Review* 10 1989: 78

for

Dewey DeWitt

who suggested this volume

Contents

"So it began"   3-15   Oestreich 1983

Preface

We have been friends since 1975 when we were introduced by a student, we both taught, who thought we might enjoy knowing each other. She was correct. We soon discovered that we had both been ΣAEs on different campuses in different decades. We have spent a great deal of time together since 1975, cross-country skiing, coaching softball, going on road trips, drinking, and talking, mostly talking. We have learned a great deal about our own craft by trying to explain to each other what we do and how we do it.

We have created projects together since 1976 when we put together our first book *The Amish: 2 Perceptions*. That was a compilation of Oestreich woodblock prints and Perkins poems. On that project we worked independently, reacting to our individual perceptions of Amish life. The next year *Billy the Kid, Chicken Gizzards and Other Tales* was published with stories by Perkins and pen and ink sketch illustrations by Oestreich. In 1977 we collaborated on *The Woodcarver, a poem* by Perkins with woodcut illustrations by Oestreich. In 1981 we made a grave mistake. By that time *The Amish: 2 Perceptions* was out of print. We decided to do a second volume, *The Amish: 2 Perceptions 2*. Oestreich, who had painted and sold three thousand eight hundred and twenty nine little Amish watercolors, was convinced that anything with the word "Amish" on it would sell like funnel cakes in the New Wilmington area. We were wrong, and we still have a number of copies of that volume with a nice centerfold farm scene by Oestreich and the fairly widely known poem "When Bill McTaggart Lost His Dog" by Perkins. In 1990 Perkins' short stories were republished in an expanded edition titled *Snakes, Butterbeans and the Discovery of Electricity*, again with Oestreich's illustrations, and in 2003 that volume was republished as a hardback volume by Mercer University Press.

We have not worked on a joint book project since the ill-fated *The Amish: 2 Perceptions 2* back in 1981. A year or so ago, Dr. Dewey DeWitt suggested that a Oestreich's bird prints should be gathered together and published. Perkins realized that over the years he had written a number of "bird" poems, and the idea for a new collaboration was born. In this work we are operating as we did in the Amish books, each of us working independently with the general notion of birds. Oestreich is interested in form and color while Perkins uses birds as metaphor. Neither of us know any more about birds than we knew about the Amish, so we asked two local ornithologists Adam and Kerri Duerr to write an introduction for this work. They agreed and, in so doing, lent some credibility to this avian treatise.

In addition to them we have a number of folks to thank for their help in realizing this project. Nelson seldom produced large numbers of any print. There were originally as many as twenty of several of the bird series. There was also only a single artist's proof of one of the prints in this volume. The prints were very popular so few of them remain in the artist's collection. We are grateful to Robert Davis, Dewey DeWitt, Eleanor DeWitt, Mark DeWitt, Fran Hackett, Don Harclerode, Kim Kaso, Joanne Morrissey, Laurie Pithian, Jack Ridl, Barbara Shetty, Susan Sholle-Martin, Angela Walker, Andrew Ade and Anne Stone who offered to trust us to reproduce their Oestreich prints.

We would like to thank *Westminster Magazine* for announcing our project, Katie Bittner of the Westminster College Audio-Visual Department for digitalizing the wood block prints, and Brian Schulz for creating mock ups of the material. And finally the very talented team of Valentine and Cassie Brkich who run Dawn Valley Press.

Nelson E. Oestreich
James A. Perkins
New Wilmington, PA
September 25, 2012

Introduction

Birds are the most obvious wild things we have around us, and from the earliest records of humankind, they have appeared as ubiquitous symbols of our everyday lives. They are much watched and much loved, by scientists, sportsmen, poets, artists and the general public alike.

Our fascination with birds centers on their unique ability to fly. Flight is central to avian adaptation. And for humans, the idea of flight serves as a link between our earth-bound lives and the upper air of possibility, between our reality and our aspiration. Hawks can dive for mammalian prey at breathtaking speeds and seem to "drop reckless onto air"; hummingbirds can hover to drink nectar from flowers, and gulls can "dart and glide" and remain airborne over the ocean in powerful winds. Some birds fly in flocks or tight aerodynamic v-shaped formations. These precise aerobatics can make even the most sophisticated aircraft seem inferior.

Some birds travel long distances during migration and are expert navigators. For example, warblers spend the winter in Central and South America and reliably return to the same breeding territories in North America each spring. The arrival of these Neotropical (from the new world tropics) migrants on northern breeding grounds signals the end of winter and the sense of renewal that comes with "thoughts of spring."

Birds are also aesthetically pleasing and highly diverse. Some birds display elaborate colors and forms that seem to defy nature. For example, the Blue-Footed Booby, a seabird common to the Galapagos Islands, Ecuador, has bright yellow eyes and large webbed feet that are a deep aquamarine color. Boobies are well-known for their courtship dance where a male will stomp and flaunt his blue feet and dance to impress a female. Many birds have vibrant colored feathers that will easily catch even an amateur's eye. The "flashy red and gold chevrons" of Red-winged blackbirds are easy to spot in marsh habitats where they nest. Like the boobies, they too use their bright-color badges to attract females for mating. Flashy colors are energetically expensive for individual birds to produce, thus only the males with the brightest feet or chest badges will attract a mate, not unlike the "upper-class men" of "senior hall."

The interest of humans with birds is as diverse as the birds themselves. They have served as religious and cultural symbols of peace and war and status, as subjects of art and poetry, and as objects for sport and for scientific study. It is not surprising that many of us are fascinated by the resemblance of the behavior of birds to our own. Birds provide a natural metaphor for the song all humans aspire to. We envy their ease of expression, and use them to voice our own concerns, joy, grief, love, comfort, survival, and freedom. It is also no surprise that poets and artists have been drawn to birds as a subject of expression of their vocations.

The modern science of ornithology was born from primitive drawings and observations of birds captured in daily journals of amateurs and early scientists like Aristotle. As descendants of dinosaurs, birds have been central to development of major theories about the formation of species and evolution. They have also played a large role in our understanding of communication and learning in animals, much of which applies to human behavior. Birds are also of central importance in our understanding of global environmental issues like the impact of human development on ecosystems, climate change, and pollution. Because they are present in all types of habitat across the globe, they serve as important indicators of the health of ecosystems. The canary in the coal mine was a real canary before it became a cliché. Bird's appeal motivates millions of people to take time to observe them, count them, care about their well-being, and act on their behalf.

The great appeal of birds has led both of us to devote our careers to the scientific study of birds. As professional ornithologists, we are interested in understanding the behaviors of individual birds and how they affect the dynamics of populations of a species. With the knowledge we gain from these studies, we can provide scientific data to others who manage habitats and populations with the goal of balancing the needs of both humans and wildlife. Although the objectives of our research are similar, we each work with different species in different ecosystems.

Kerri has primarily worked with small songbird species. For example, she studied Black-throated Blue Warblers on their summer breeding grounds in the forests of the Green Mountains in Vermont. These are small birds (weighing only 5 grams – about the weight of a nickel coin in your hand) that spend winters in the western Antilles and migrate to eastern North America in the summer to nest in large areas of forest. Many populations of Neotropical migrants, like warblers, are experiencing severe declines in number, mainly as a result of habitat loss and degradation. As forests are cleared for agriculture and timber extraction, it is unclear how warbler breeding success and survival will be affected, and whether individuals will be able to adjust to changes in their habitat, both in the short term, and over longer evolutionary time periods.

Kerri also works with Eastern Bluebirds. In the past, Bluebirds experienced severe population declines as a result of pesticide use by humans (DDT) and loss of habitat for nesting. In response, biologists and citizens have established nest box trails throughout the U.S. in hopes of proving safe nesting areas and helping populations recover. In recent years, as a result of federal regulations to ban DDT and mitigating habitat loss with nest sites, populations have begun to recover. However, many habitats where nest boxes have been placed are threatened by human activity. For example, golf courses, roadsides, and backyards provide ideal habitat for bluebirds that prefer habitat edges, but are impacted by mowing activity, recreational use, and traffic. In housing developments, house cats that are let outside are common predator that can have negative impact on nesting birds in some areas. Kerri's research questions whether habitats she believes ideal for bluebirds really benefit the birds' ability to survive and reproduce. To investigate these questions, she captures and marks individuals with unique characters so that she can track them over time to estimate how long they live, how many offspring they produce, and how they respond to their environment. To mark them, she attaches unique combinations of colored bracelets to their legs, and a single aluminum band with a unique number distributed by the U.S. Fish and Wildlife Service. She can use information from this research to educate habitat managers and citizens about where nest box trails would be most beneficial for bluebirds and other species that use nest boxes (e.g. House Wrens and Chickadees).

Adam generally works with larger birds like Double-crested Cormorants, Turkey Vultures, and Golden Eagles. He captures individuals of each species and marks them. Cormorants wear leg bands with a 3-digit combination of letters and numbers, vultures have cattle ear tags on their wings that are numbered, and eagles carry transmitters that record their location using Global Positioning Systems, and computer servers communicate bird locations through cell phone networks. With cormorants and vultures, Adam has shown that when individuals are removed from a habitat (either because they die or are exterminated by wildlife managers), other individuals of the same species respond by leaving the habitat. He likens this to people leaving a bad neighborhood when crime rates increase. He can use information about where birds spend their time and how they respond to changes in habitat to manage habitat for the needs of wildlife and humans. For example, in water bodies in eastern North America cormorant populations have so severely increased in number that in some locations they have altered habitats and become a nuisance for humans. They build nests in trees on islands, and where breeding densities are high they can destroy the vegetation and displace other water birds that use the same habitat. By following individuals, wildlife managers can employ techniques to manage local population sizes. Vultures, like cormorants (and humans) are also social creatures, often congregating in large numbers in some habitats shared by humans. They are known to eat rubber, including windshield wipers on cars, and they defecate on man-made structures (e.g. a power plant in Virginia).

In recent years, scientific evidence for global warming and climate change has led to an increase in the development of alternative clean energy sources. Development of habitat for wind farms is one area that has received much attention and it is becoming increasingly unclear what effects wind turbines can have on bird populations in certain areas. Adam studies flight behavior by eagles to determine factors that may influence how and where individuals fly; whether to flap or soar, follow a ridgeline, or head out over a valley. Detailed understanding of flight behavior will allow us to help manage how and where wind farms are built and to prevent collisions of eagles, and other birds, with turbines.   As we develop knowledge about bird populations and ecology, we continue to be fascinated by individuals and enjoy sharing this fascination with others. We also love to see and hear other people's perspectives on birds, as this expands our own views.

Even a book open in the hand looks like a bird in flight. In *Bird by Bird Watching*, the reader will discover the fascinating diversity of birds, their behaviors, and their power over the human spirit.

Kerri Cornell Duerr & Adam E. Duerr

"Bird Series #8"   14-18   Otto Smith '77'

Almost Still Life

The only thing moving
In the whole landscape
Is the eye of the kingfisher?
Perched in the breathless
Pine watching the gray
Flat waters of the lake
Making this perilous territory
For the fingerling bass
Hanging still in the shallows
Near the black rock
Under the low sky.

"Bird Series #7"   1-18   Oestreich '77

Encounter in a Wind Gust

*Name a redbird. If you make a wish before
the bird flies away, it will come true*

Daniel Thomas, *Kentucky Superstitions*

Past me,
Blown by a gust
Of chill, damp December wind,
A red leaf
Too large to be a sumac
Fluttered clumsily and settled by my walk.
Then,
When the wind paused,
The leaf flew off
Making a cardinal's cry.

"Pigeon" 8-9 Oestreich '06

Who We Are

An armored thing
Almost prehistoric
Too slow for this modern pace

       I am a turtle
Who tried to cross
All the expressway lanes

       Now I lie
On the road's shoulder
My shell shattered

    By a southbound truck
You are a crow
Who sweeps down

    When the traffic allows
To pick at my flesh
Soft pink exposed

    With your ceaseless cry
I love you
I love you.

"I Walk through the Cornfield with the Mysterious Pheasant"

Bird Dog

You will have bad luck if you break a bird's egg.

Mountain Superstition

Ahead of me
Too close to the road
A large red dog
Crouches
Still.

As I pass by
I see the swollen stomach
Fixed eyes flies circling
Bloody
Flesh.

In the mirror
I take a last look as the high sweet
Stench sucks the good air out and my
Stomach
Knots.

On down the road
I remember a covey of quail
Flushed by my mowing machine
From their
Shells
Ten years before
The big red dog scented them
Pointed toward death and sunk to his
Final
Crouch

"Bird Series #13"   1"19   Oeser Melson 97'

Dalliance

Dear witch, dear devious dove,
I halfway know the meaning
Of these giddy spirallings.

Theodore Roethke, *Straw for the Fire*

Higher than the single heart can soar
We rise riding the heat
Of our own need
To devour, claw,
Entangle, and cry out
Then fall
Haggard
In a helical embrace
Toward death
Only to veer
And ride tired wings
Apart
To more common violence

"Bird Series #9 - Variation #2"   1-B   Oshutsiah '77'

Going Long Distances

Sleeping with One Eye Open

Mark Strand

Sometimes truckers
Going coast to coast
Push too hard
Fake their logs
And slam their rigs
Into the abutments
Of dreams.
On interstates
Drunk with fatigue
I've snapped awake
With the taste of fear
Rising in my throat
Unable to remember
The last five miles.
Migrating birds drop off
On their long flights
Glide through clouds
Smash into sunshine
And awaken
With no idea where
Off earth they are

"Bird Series #5- Prairie Chicken"   13-20   Oestreich '77

Hawks Drop Reckless Onto Air

Hawks watchful
In the tops
Of barren trees
Seem
      to
      fall
          into flight
Their frightful claws
Release the limb
They drop reckless
Onto the air
Caught in the curve
Of their wide wings

      Then they swoop
At terrific speed
Toward something
We cannot see
Moving against the snow

      Hawks eat everything

       Skin scale
Fur flesh
Feathers
Bone
And throw up
What they can't digest

      Hawks do not sing

"Bird Series #3"   15-17   Oestreich '77'

Thoughts of Spring, in a Field in Kentucky

Transients arrive in middle or late February

Kentucky Birds: a Finding Guide

They came suddenly.
I turned my head at the sound
Of so many wings,
And there they were
Foraging in the bare field,
Hundreds of Grackles
Rising, wheeling, dropping again
As one, like a church choir.
Iridescent black
Like a silken Gypsy scarf,
They rode the wind
To a huge, solitary, leafless oak
Back-lighted by the afternoon sun.
They rested in the grey matter
Of the ancient oak
Like bad habits.
Then they rose
Shimmered in the sun
And veered away
Like a February thought of spring.

"Proud Cock"

12-10

Oestruch '67'

Invisible Deaths

During the winter
In the woods
Things happen
At night
When no one is watching

    Wind-blown branches
Snapping in the cold
Lie across the tracks
Your skiis made
Yesterday

    This is the way
Trees die
Twig by twig
Branch by branch
In the wind and cold

    You
Have never seen
A bird die in flight
And arc
Like a feathered stone

    In your house
Most of the dust
Is dead skin
Sloughed off
When you were not watching

"Bird Series #4"   18-19   Ostreich '77'

Except for the Gull

A tropical storm
Building toward hurricane
Crashes the Outer Banks.
High winds
Drive the shorebirds
To shelter
Except for the gull
That fights
Darts and glides
Adapting to adversity
Turning the storm
Into a concerto
For two wings
Unaccompanied

"Bird Series #10"   14-19   Oestreich '97

The Sound of My Brush

The gull drifts seaward
On still wings.
The sun is tied
By a silver rope
To the water of the lake.
For hours now
Nothing has moved.
The sound of my brush
Rubbing the ink stone
Frightens the sparrow
In the blue spruce
By the cliff.

Remembering the Field of Blackbirds

I. Honking madly, geese woke me
    From a dream of grid-locked traffic
    To a dawn full of change. They left
    Before the season's first sleet
    Rattled through oak leaves
    That will hang on till spring.
    Now, surprised grackles cloak the pines
    Across the street like a noisy shroud.

II. They say the birds tore at the bodies
     Of the dead for weeks in 1389.
     After the Battle of Kosovo Polje
     Where South Slavs met Ottoman Turks.
     So many died on both sides
     The living could not bury the dead.
     They called it *The Field of Blackbirds*.

III. Blood soaks that land again
      Serbs and Croats, released
      From the dream of Communism,
      Are awake to whatever nightmare
      Exploded into World War I.

IV. In western Pennsylvania, old neighbors,
     Second generation Yugoslavs
     Whose parents fled the horror and met
     In backyards over sausages and beer
     To denounce the Communists in tongues
     They will carry to their graves,
     Devour the news from their homelands,
     Study maps that change daily,
     Learn to hate each other
     And fall into fist fights
     In their local Serbo-Croatian clubs.

V.   The cold.
     The cold is upon us,
     And the blackbirds
     Wait in the pines across the street
     Wait as though something,
     Something that glides across
     Landscape and time,
     Through the collective memory
     Of ravens, awakens.

"High Rides The Queen"   7-15   Oestreich '70

The Possibility of the Lesser Blue Heron

The lesser blue heron
Did not care
Above the waterline
About your moans
Or my ragged breath,
While we struggled
To gain and lose
Over the know territory
Of our warm damp flesh.
He moved
With stately step and slow
Like a monarch in progress
Half way around the lake
Never taking his eye
Off the least possibility

"Bird Series #14 - Rock Bird"   12-16   Oestreich '77'

Searching for Blue

We roll south in search of blue
While the Lake Erie Storm Track
Covers western PA with a blanket
Of thick gray batting.

      Nelson sees a blue bird
Flit into a roadside pine.
But that is precious little blue,
And the horizon is a solder strip
Holding the gun-metal gray sky
To the dead-grass brown earth.

     Miles and miles of pine trees
Close in like the pines of I-80.
Except for the fish stew
And that brown pelican
Working the chum
Behind a fishing scow
We might as well be at Isaly's

"Bird Series #12 - Juncos and Sunflower Seeds"   11-20   Oestreich "77"

Precision Aerobatics

Flocks of birds in flight
Change direction more suddenly
Than cries could cause
More uniformly
Than sight would allow.

      They move as one
Like dancers
In a finale
Or a sail
Caught by the wind.

      Static charges cover
Each bird's body
Making the flock
An electromagnetic field.

      Fluctuations flash
Across this field
At the speed of light.

      These may explain
Breath-taking maneuvers
In precise formation
Against a background
Of blue.

"Bird Series #1"   8-19   Oestreich '99

Bird Dreams

(for Sarah)

Avian physiologists wire
The brains of birds
Threading stainless steel screws
Into their skulls
To chart the storms
Of sleep.
Penguins, pigeons, owls
Jackdaws, hawks, and starlings
Exhibit paradoxical sleep,
Short electrical bursts of up to 60 Hertz,
Brief periods of rapid eye movement
When they may be dreaming
Of shaking hands
        at the Rotary meeting
Of taking the Amtrak
        Auto-Train to Florida
Of wearing sneakers and jogging
        around the block
Of cooking worms
        on the backyard grill
Of lying in the psychoanalyst's couch
        telling about their dreams

"Hummingbird"   Studio Proof (18)   Oehlschlager 1982

Remembering Through the Blood

Hafiz, if you desire her presence, never leave her. When you find the one you seek, abandon the world and let it go.

Hafiz-i Shirazi, GHAZAL I

Hawks held
Too long in hand
Doubt their wings
For extended flight,
But their blood remembers
Updrafts
And the weight of sky.
Finally unhooded
They lift off
The gauntlet
Jesses dangling
To soar beyond
Recall.
Learning to hold you
I study letting go.

"Moon Bird"   8-8   Ott Reich '74

Breakfast Interruptus

At breakfast,
Eggs over easy
And a side of bacon,
I was stopped
By a sound
I could not recognize,
Sustained, high and inhuman,
A shriek.

       Beyond the glass
A Junko, caught
In the talons
Of a Harris Hawk,
Twisting and screaming
As the hawk
Pulled living flesh
From fragile bone.

       I could not look away
Before the angel of death
Lifted off leaving
Against the snow
Not blood or flesh or bone
But a ring of slate grey feathers
And wing prints
Surrounding an awful emptiness.

       My egg was cold;
The yellow congealed
On the plate,
The white shading
Toward grey.

The Revenge of the Blue Booby

(for James Tate)

I. Just at sundown
    One muggy day
    Last summer
    You were looking for Algeria—
    A blue notebook
    You carried there—
    I was looking
    For something to do.
    We outboarded Saranac Lake
    Into a thunder storm—
    Like those absolute fools
    We'd denied being
    To wives, friends,
    Fellow faculty members,
    And psychiatrists for years—
    Toward the island
    Where we never found
    Your notebook.

II. I lived to tell about it
    To my class this spring
    Studying your poem
    About the strange dull birds
    Of Galapogos
    (which the Norton
    Wrongly places
    In the Caribbean).
    It was then I knew,
    But I needed proof.

III. Yesterday I checked
    At the airport
    In Saranac Lake.
    "Sure, mister. I remember him.
    Odd, little guy, sunglasses,
    Trench coat, walked funny,
    Ugliest nose I ever saw.
    But that's not why I remember.
    No sir! It was where he was going.
    Only man ever flew from here
    Ticketed to Ecuador.

"Bird Series #6"   16-20   Oelofreich '77

Cape Fear River Pie

(for Tommy)

On Striking Island
Ibis explode
Like popcorn
Out of the tree line
Sometimes
           here
Sometimes
           there

    Rising up and floating back
Until something stirs them all
And they rise as a cloud
In a winged moil
To float like meringue
Above the brown of the sand
And the green of the trees
Turning the whole island
Into a slice of pie.

Dressing the Bride of Spring

From a distance
Like a bride's veil
Or that light canvas
That covers tobacco beds
They floated
Behind the disc harrow
Across the spring field

      Close enough to hear
The strain of that John Deere
We could hear them too
A shrill confusion
And see the thick moil
Dive and scramble
Of sea gulls
Feasting
On the grubs and worms
In the harrow's wake.

"Goose"   4-10   Olshtuch 1979

A Poem About
a Goose

(for Jane)

You came into the bedroom
After taking the kid to school
Excited about Canada Geese
On the lake
Lots of them
They're so big
There are so many of them.

        I was still in bed
Tired bored or mad
About something, as usual.
I didn't say a thing
You stood by the window
And went on about the geese
Until my lack of response
Froze you mid-sentence
And you said
Well, I have things to do.

        I have things to do, too
And one of them is to thank you
For telling me about the geese.
You told about them well.
I saw them float
Still and white across my mind
And they were lovely.

Looking is Important: Finding Isn't

A turtle-dove's cry on the first day of the year means a good crop year

Western Kentucky Superstition

I. In *Walden*
Henry Thoreau says
Somewhere years ago
He lost a hound
A bay horse
And a turtle dove
Says he followed them for years
Asked folks he met
About that hound
That bay horse
And that turtle dove
Says he *met one or two*
Who had heard the hound
And the tramp of the horse
And even seen the dove
Disappear behind a cloud.
He never found them.
Though he was no worse off
For having made his search.

II. Since then critics have tried to find
What Thoreau really lost.
"A hound?
A bay horse
And a turtle dove?
Be serious now.
He *must* have meant something else."
It may be that bird.
Critics can't imagine Thoreau
Tramping around Concord
Looking for a turtle dove.
I had a friend once lost his dog
And spent the summer
On dirt back roads
Going door to door
Showing farmers photos
Of his pooch.
He never found his dog

III. But felt better for his search.
Chances are for Thoreau
There was no hound
No bay horse and no turtle dove.
But if you're out walking
In places you're not known
You ain't from around here
Are you boy?
It's best to tell the locals
Something they'll believe.
A hound
A bay horse
And a turtle dove
Sound better on the local ear
Than some abstraction,
Angst or fear.
Got a place out by Walden,
The pond, you know.
Borrowed an axe and built it
With my own two hands.
Now I'm out walking
Sort of searching for myself.
This is not what the locals
Want to hear.

IV. The hound
The bay horse
And the turtle dove
Which never did exist
Can hardly stand
For anything at all.
(Jacque Derrida
Would appreciate
This *differ( )nce.*)
But their absence made them real.
And those Thoreau met
Seemed as anxious to recover them
As if they had lost them themselves.
Remember Henry also said
There should be ponds
Whose bottoms are not known.
We may never find one.
But even if no such ponds exist,
We'll all be better
For having made the search.

"Bird Series #2"   11-16   Otostretch 77

Red-winged Blackbirds/ May 2009

Upper-class men
stuff freshman boys
into lockers
then glide
down Senior Hall
flashing
red and gold chevrons
on their black letter jackets
to impress girls
dreaming of nests
in the Cattail marsh

About the Artist

NELSON OESTREICH former professor and chair of the Department of Art at Westminster College, New Wilmington, PA, held B.S. and M.F.A. degrees from Bowling Green University and an M.A. from Kent State University.

Although he concentrated on woodcuts, the form represented in this volume, he was a versatile artist who sculpted in wood, metal and stone, and painted in acrylics, oils, and watercolors.

He exhibited widely in local, regional and national shows and collected many awards. Several of his prints were reproduced in magazines. His work may be found in many public and private collections including the Butler Institute of American Art, Bowling Green State University, The Hoyt Institute of Fine Arts, Massillon Museum, Arms Museum, and Westminster College.

He collaborated with the author of this volume on six previous volumes: *The Amish: 2 Perceptions (1976), Billy the Kid, Chicken Gizzards, and Other Tales (1977), The Woodcarver (1978), The Amish: 2 Perceptions 2 (1981), Snakes, Butterbeans and the Discovery of Electricity (1990), and Snakes, Butterbeans and the Discovery of Electricity (2003). In addition he authored and illustrated Amish Children: What They Learn (1985).*

About the Author

JAMES A. PERKINS, former professor and chair of the Department of English and Public Relations at Westminster College, New Wilmington, PA, holds a B.A. from Centre College, an M.A. from Miami University, and a Ph.D. from The University of Tennessee.

In addition to the volumes on which he collaborated with Nelson Oestreich, he has published more than a hundred short stories and poems in little and literary magazines including *Black Fly Review, Cape Rock, the Southern Review, Colorado Review,* and Antigonish Review. From 1974 to 1979, he attended all six *fiction international*/St. Lawrence University Writers' Conferences near Saranac Lake, NY.

On five occasions he was a fellow in an NEH Summer Seminar at Princeton, NYU or Yale. The last of these with R.W.B. Liewis at Yale led Perkins to the work of Robert Penn Warren on whom he has since written or edited six books including the final four of the six volume *Selected Letters of Robert Penn Warren.* He has also published books on Robert Drake, David Madden and various other Southern Writers.

He was a Fulbright Senior Lecturer at Seoul National University in 1998, an experience that led to his collaboration on *Brother Enemy: Poems of the Korean War,* and he was given Westminster College's Distinguished Faculty Award in 2006.

About the Ornithologists

KERRI CORNELL DUERR is an Assistant Professor of Biology at Westminster College in New Wilmington, Pennsylvania. She became interested in an ornithology career as an undergraduate student at Hartwick College where she studied migratory forest songbirds in upstate New York, USA and San Salvador, Bahamas. Following graduation, her passions for island and forest ecology led her to pursue an opportunity to study birds in Hawaii, where she monitored populations of endangered Hawaiian Honeycreepers in the rainforests of Hakalau National Wildlife Refuge on the Big Island. Realizing she missed the temperate forests of the northeast US, she returned to work for Dartmouth College on a project monitoring long-term population trends of Black-throated blue warblers at the Hubbard Brook Experimental Forest in New Hampshire. She later earned a Master of Science degree in Biology at Villanova University where she combined field work and molecular ecology to investigate the reproductive consequences of hybridization between Carolina and Black-capped chickadees in southeastern Pennsylvania. Kerri earned a Doctorate of Philosophy in Natural Resources from the University of Vermont. For her dissertation research, she studied how forest fragmentation impacted reproductive success and annual survival of Black-throated blue warblers in Green Mountain National Forest. In further pursuit of her interest in understanding how habitat degradation by humans impacts reproduction and survival of bird species, she conducted research as a post-doctoral scientist at both the University of Missouri, studying the threated Cerulean Warbler in central and eastern USA, and at the College of William and Mary, studying impacts of golf courses on populations of Eastern bluebirds. She is published in the journals *Landscape Ecology*, *Molecular Ecology*, *Journal of Field Ornithology*, and *The Auk*, and is a member of the American Ornithologists' Union.

ADAM DUERR is an Adjunct Assistant Professor in the Division of Forestry and Natural Resources at West Virginia University. He became interested in wildlife while deer hunting with his father in the Blue Wilderness area in Arizona, where Mexican Wolves have been reintroduced. He shifted his interest to research during a summer job working for a graduate student and radio tracking Northern Goshawks. He continued working for graduate students studying birds in Arizona, including Elegant Trogons, Masked Bobwhite Quail, Cooper's Hawks, and Gray Hawks while completing his Bachelors of Science degree in Wildlife and Fisheries Management and before beginning his Masters of Science degree, both at the University of Arizona. His master's thesis investigated the abundance of lead fishing tackle in the environment relative to lead poisoning of water birds in the United States. While doing field work for his thesis, Adam drove to each of the corners of the continental United States collecting data and seeing the wide variety of bird life throughout the USA. After completing his first graduate degree, he worked for two years as an environmental consultant in Tucson, Arizona, his home town. He then moved to Burlington, Vermont to work on his Doctor of Philosophy at the University of Vermont. For his dissertation, he studied population growth, population control, and management of Double-Crested Cormorants on Lake Champlain. After completing his dissertation, he moved to the College of William and Mary in Virginia. Over the next three years, he worked on several research projects that focused on Double-crested Cormorants, Brown Pelicans, Osprey, Bald Eagles, Black Vultures, Red Knots, Whimbrel, and American Oystercatchers. Adam then moved to Western Pennsylvania and works at the University of West Virginia, where he works with a team of biologists that study Golden Eagle movements and the risks that renewable energy such as wind energy and solar energy pose to the eagles. He is a member of several professional organizations including The Wildlife Society, Raptor Research Foundation, The Waterbird Society, and Cooper Ornithological Society. Adam has published in *Journal of Great Lakes Research*, *Journal of Wildlife Management*, *PLoS One (Public Library of Science)*, *Southwestern Naturalist*, *Wader Study Group Bulletin*, *Waterbirds*, and the *Wildlife Society Bulletin*.

About the Designer

ANNA BUZZELLI has always wanted to be an artist. Growing up, she'd spend countless hours drawing and painting, experimenting with different media, color combinations, and textures. This passion led her to Carlow University and The Art Institute of Pittsburgh, where she studied graphic design. After graduating, she worked as a freelancer before joining an agency just outside of Pittsburgh where she honed her craft working with all types of businesses from startups to Fortune 500s. In 2010, she launched Buzzelli Design—a creative graphic design and web development shop. Over the past 10+ years, Anna has used her skills to craft memorable advertisements, magazines, mobile websites, book covers, logos and more.

www.ingramcontent.com/pod-product-compliance
Lightning Source LLC
Chambersburg PA
CBHW040915100426
42737CB00042B/89